STRUCTURAL WONDERS
TAJ MAHAL

by Ashley Gish

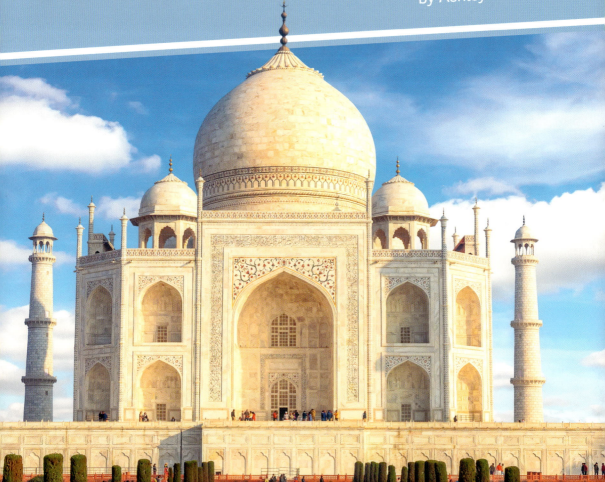

WWW.FOCUSREADERS.COM

Copyright © 2023 by Focus Readers®, Lake Elmo, MN 55042. All rights reserved. No part of this book may be reproduced or utilized in any form or by any means without written permission from the publisher.

Focus Readers is distributed by North Star Editions:
sales@northstareditions.com | 888-417-0195

Produced for Focus Readers by Red Line Editorial.

Photographs ©: Shutterstock Images, cover, 1, 4–5, 7, 10–11, 13, 15, 17, 21, 24–25, 27, 29; Dinodia Photos RM/Alamy, 8; Fine Art Images/Heritage Images/Hulton Archive/Getty Images, 18–19; Lucas Vallecillos/VW Pics/AP Images, 23

Library of Congress Cataloging-in-Publication Data
Names: Gish, Ashley, author.
Title: Taj Mahal / Ashley Gish.
Description: Lake Elmo : Focus Readers, 2023. | Series: Structural wonders
  | Includes index. | Audience: Grades 4-6
Identifiers: LCCN 2022033734 (print) | LCCN 2022033735 (ebook) | ISBN
  9781637394823 (hardcover) | ISBN 9781637395196 (paperback) | ISBN
  9781637395882 (pdf) | ISBN 9781637395561 (ebook)
Subjects: LCSH: Taj Mahal (Agra, India)--Juvenile literature. |
  Architecture, Mogul Empire--India--Agra--Juvenile literature. | Agra
  (India)--Buildings, structures, etc.--Juvenile literature.
Classification: LCC NA6183 .G57 2023 (print) | LCC NA6183 (ebook) | DDC
  726/.809542--dc23/eng/20220720
LC record available at https://lccn.loc.gov/2022033734
LC ebook record available at https://lccn.loc.gov/2022033735

Printed in the United States of America
Mankato, MN
012023

ABOUT THE AUTHOR
Ashley Gish earned her degree in creative writing from Minnesota State University, Mankato. She has authored more than 60 juvenile nonfiction books. Ashley lives happily in Rochester, Minnesota, with her husband, daughter, dog, cat, and three chickens.

TABLE OF CONTENTS

CHAPTER 1
The Jewel of India 5

CHAPTER 2
A Marble Masterpiece 11

THAT'S AMAZING!
Many Materials 16

CHAPTER 3
Taj Mahal History 19

CHAPTER 4
Protecting the Site 25

Focus on the Taj Mahal • 30
Glossary • 31
To Learn More • 32
Index • 32

CHAPTER 1

THE JEWEL OF INDIA

Excited **tourists** step into horse-drawn carriages. The carriages are decorated with flowers and bells. The horses trot down the busy street. Soon, the tourists arrive at a huge gate. It is made of red sandstone. The visitors walk through the gate. They admire the beautiful carvings of flowers.

Visitors pass through a large sandstone gate before entering the Taj Mahal.

Finally, the tourists get their first view of the Taj Mahal. Its onion-shaped dome glows pink in the morning light. Four smaller domes surround the main dome. At the corners of the building stand four towers. They are called minarets. A long pool reflects the Taj Mahal's beauty. The tourists walk through the gardens. They are eager to get a closer look.

The Taj Mahal is located in Agra, India. The building is not a temple or palace. It is a **mausoleum**. The Taj Mahal sits in the middle of a 42-acre (17-ha) site. The site also features a **mosque** and a guest house. Behind these structures is the Yamuna River.

The Taj Mahal appears to change color over the course of the day.

    The Taj Mahal is known as a symbol of love. Shah Jahan ruled northern India in the 1600s. He adored his wife

  A painting shows Mumtaz Mahal and Shah Jahan smelling roses.

Mumtaz Mahal. Sadly, she died giving birth. But she shared a last wish with her husband. She wanted him to build her a beautiful mausoleum. The heartbroken ruler agreed. He ordered the Taj Mahal to be built. Both he and Mumtaz Mahal are buried beneath it.

The Taj Mahal is one of the New Seven Wonders of the World. It is also a World Heritage Site. That means many people agree it is an important part of human history. Experts consider the Taj Mahal one of the greatest examples of **architecture** in the world.

THE MUGHAL EMPIRE

The Mughal Empire took control of northern India in the early 1500s. Its leaders were related to the famous warrior Genghis Khan. The Mughals thrived for many years. However, the empire also dealt with frequent wars. Shah Jahan ruled the Mughal Empire from 1628 to 1658. He loved architecture. The Taj Mahal, Pearl Mosque, Great Mosque, and Red Fort were all built at his command.

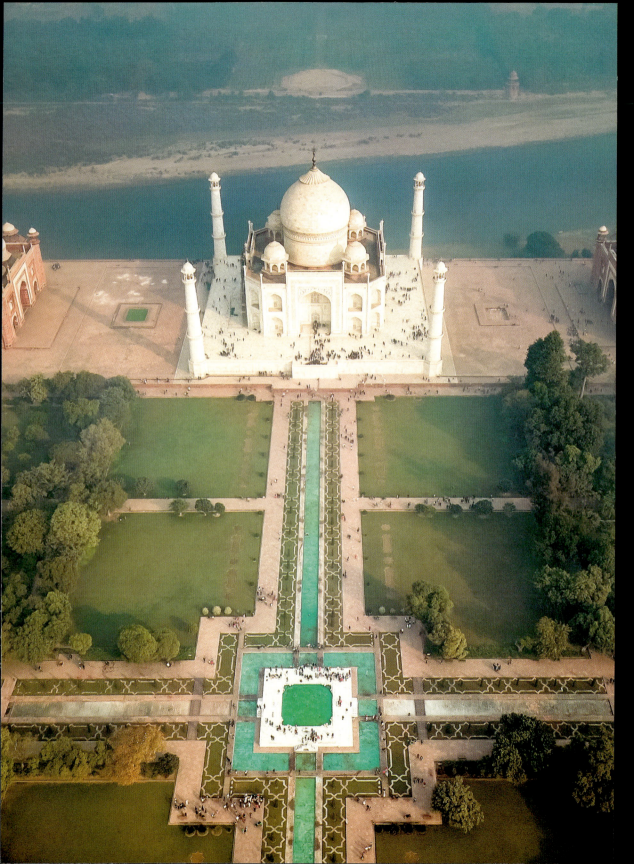

CHAPTER 2

A MARBLE MASTERPIECE

Work on the Taj Mahal began in 1632. The mausoleum took 17 years to build. It took five additional years to finish everything else at the site. More than 20,000 builders worked on the structure. More than 1,000 elephants helped, too. The animals carried materials from all over Asia. These materials

Ustad Ahmad Lahori was the Taj Mahal's lead architect.

included marble, sandstone, and various kinds of gems.

The Taj Mahal's architects used many different styles and designs. The mausoleum itself is made of white marble. However, its color appears to change. It varies based on the angle of the sunlight. The top of the main dome is

TAJ MAHAL COPYCATS

People have built look-alikes of the Taj Mahal all over the world. For example, a palace in England shares many of the Taj Mahal's design **elements**. In 2021, a man in India built a house that looks like the Taj Mahal. A man in California even built a houseboat in the style of the Taj Mahal.

The Taj Mahal's brass finial rises to a height of 240 feet (73 m).

shaped like a lotus flower. This flower is used in religious decorations throughout India. It is a symbol of rebirth. A pole stands on top of the dome. This pole is called a finial. It displays a crescent moon. That is a symbol of Islam.

Inside the mausoleum, there is one main room. There are also several smaller rooms. Mumtaz Mahal and Shah Jahan's cenotaphs are in the main room. Cenotaphs are stone boxes. They are made to look like tombs. However, they do not contain human remains. Mumtaz Mahal and Shah Jahan are actually buried under the mausoleum.

The other rooms in the Taj Mahal are empty. Their walls are covered in decorative stones. Words from the **Quran** are carved on the walls.

The mosque sits to the west of the Taj Mahal. The guest house is to the east. Both buildings are made of red sandstone. This material was common for buildings in the Mughal Empire. The two buildings look similar to each other. Each building has domes that match the Taj Mahal's. **Muslims** use the mosque for prayer. In the past, visitors may have stayed in the guest house. However, people aren't allowed to stay there today.

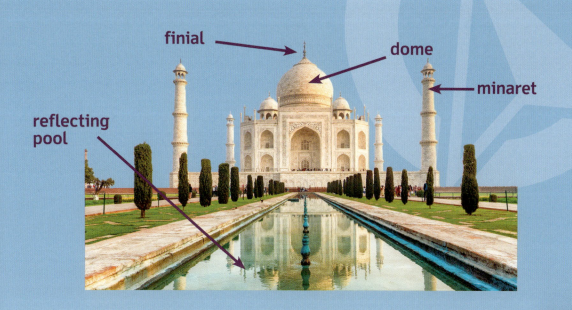

TAJ MAHAL FEATURES

THAT'S AMAZING!

MANY MATERIALS

Building materials for the Taj Mahal came from all over Asia. Bricks were produced in Agra. The red sandstone was also cut near Agra. However, most of the decorative stones came from farther away. These stones included jade and crystal from China. Turquoise was brought from Tibet. And sapphires were brought from Sri Lanka.

The white marble came from Makrana, India. Makrana marble is known as Sang-e-Marmar. This comes from a Persian phrase meaning "flawless white marble." The distance from Makrana to Agra is approximately 240 miles (390 km). Hundreds of carts made this long journey. Stonecutters in Makrana stayed busy for many years while the Taj Mahal was being built.

Arabic writing made of black marble is built into the Taj Mahal's interior walls.

CHAPTER 3

TAJ MAHAL HISTORY

People have lived in the Agra area for thousands of years. However, the city wasn't officially founded until 1504. Agra served as the capital of the Mughal Empire from 1526 until 1658. During that time, the Mughals built beautiful gardens and a fort. The city became known for art, religion, and trading. The city's

Many beautiful works of art were produced in the Mughal Empire.

role changed over time. However, it has remained a popular destination in India.

Western tourists began visiting Agra in the 1800s. They loved the city's architecture. But soon, they started ruining the Taj Mahal. Some visitors stole gems off the walls. Others broke

MANY RULERS

A Muslim ruler named Sikandar Lodi founded Agra in 1504. After his death, his son ruled the city until 1526. This is when the Mughal Empire took over. In the 1700s, the Maratha Empire gained control of Agra. And in 1803, British **colonists** took over most of India. This included Agra. The British ruled until 1947. That year, India became an **independent** nation.

Gems create decorations of flowers on the walls of the Taj Mahal.

off pieces of marble to sell. By the late 1800s, the Taj Mahal's gardens were overgrown. The British ruler of India wanted to restore the site. Workers made the gardens look neat and tidy. They also fixed the broken stone.

Soon after, **archaeologists** began studying the Taj Mahal. The site was restored, and it remained beautiful for many years. Over time, however, the city became more modern. Factories and cars filled the sky with pollution. It formed yellow and black stains on the Taj Mahal's white marble. Meanwhile, people threw garbage into the river behind the site.

By the 2020s, more than two million people lived in Agra. Many of these people earn money working around the Taj Mahal. Some sell shirts or postcards. Others take tourists to the site.

Modern Agra is a busy city that draws tourists from around the world.

Some people drive electric cars. Others drive horse-drawn carriages or bicycle carts. Locals also relax in the Taj Mahal's gardens. And Muslims still visit the mosque to pray.

CHAPTER 4

PROTECTING THE SITE

The Taj Mahal is a major source of income for the city of Agra. Millions of people visit the Taj Mahal every year. They bring in hundreds of millions of Indian rupees. That is millions of US dollars. Some of this money is spent on fixing the Taj Mahal itself. The money is also spent on upgrades.

Workers put up scaffolding to clean the walls of the Taj Mahal.

These include new drinking fountains and air-conditioned rooms.

The Taj Mahal is in a protected zone. People must follow certain rules in this zone. These rules help protect the Taj Mahal from pollution. For instance, factories that burn coal cannot be built in the zone. Also, vehicles that use gasoline cannot enter parts of the zone.

Garbage in the Yamuna River also causes problems for the Taj Mahal. Many small fish used to live in the river. These fish ate insects called midges. However, the river is now filled with trash. This has killed many of the fish. As a result, there are not enough fish to eat the midges.

Trash along the Yamuna River affects Agra's air quality.

So, the insects gather at the Taj Mahal. Their waste turns the mausoleum green. Scientists are trying to find ways to get rid of the insects.

Shah Jahan may not have planned for his wife's mausoleum to become a tourist site. Even so, the money that the

MUD BATH

Scientists started a big cleanup project in 1994. They wanted to make the Taj Mahal as white as it was in the 1640s. Workers began smearing mud on the mausoleum. This mud is made from clay called fuller's earth. The mud soaks up grease and stains. When workers wash it off the marble, the stains come off, too. As of 2022, the project was still going. The dome was the last part left to clean.

Tourists cover their shoes inside the Taj Mahal so they won't damage the marble floor.

Taj Mahal generates is good for the city of Agra. Scientists and tourists alike want to protect the site. That way, people can enjoy the Taj Mahal for many years to come.

FOCUS ON
THE TAJ MAHAL

Write your answers on a separate piece of paper.

1. Write a letter to a friend describing the main ideas of Chapter 2.

2. Do you think Agra is doing enough to control pollution around the Taj Mahal? Why or why not?

3. Which building is used for prayer?

    A. the mausoleum
    B. the mosque
    C. the guest house

4. What is most likely to happen if factories burn coal near the Taj Mahal?

    A. More factory workers would visit the Taj Mahal.
    B. The Taj Mahal would be stained from smoke.
    C. More insects would gather near the Taj Mahal.

Answer key on page 32.

GLOSSARY

archaeologists
People who study the ancient past, often by digging up buildings or objects from long ago.

architecture
The art of designing and constructing buildings.

colonists
People who settle in a new place and take control.

elements
The basic parts of something.

independent
Able to make decisions without being controlled by another government.

mausoleum
A large building where people are buried.

mosque
A building where Muslims pray.

Muslims
People who follow the religion of Islam.

Quran
The main religious text of Islam.

tourists
People who visit an area for fun or enjoyment.

TO LEARN MORE

BOOKS

Doeden, Matt. *Travel to India*. Minneapolis: Lerner Publications, 2022.

Green, Sara. *The Taj Mahal*. Minneapolis: Bellwether Media, 2021.

Murray, Laura K. *Engineering the Taj Mahal*. Minneapolis: Abdo Publishing, 2018.

NOTE TO EDUCATORS

Visit www.focusreaders.com to find lesson plans, activities, links, and other resources related to this title.

INDEX

Agra, India, 6, 16, 19–20, 22, 25, 29
architecture, 6, 9, 12–15, 20
Asia, 11, 16

gardens, 6, 19, 21–23
gems, 12, 14, 16, 20

Islam, 13, 15, 20, 23

materials, 11–12, 14, 16
minaret, 6
mosque, 6, 9, 14–15, 23
Mughal Empire, 9, 14, 19–20
Mumtaz Mahal, 8, 14

pollution, 22, 26, 28
preservation, 25–26, 28–29

Quran, 14

Shah Jahan, 7, 9, 14, 28

tourism, 5–6, 15, 20, 22–23, 25, 28–29

World Heritage Site, 9

Yamuna River, 6, 22, 26

Answer Key: 1. Answers will vary; 2. Answers will vary; 3. B; 4. B